COLOUR BY NUMBERS

RELAXING PATTERNS

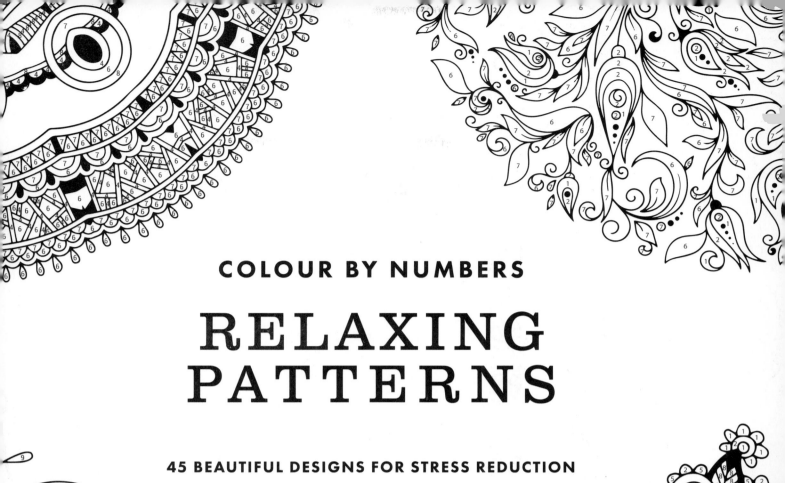

COLOUR BY NUMBERS

RELAXING PATTERNS

45 BEAUTIFUL DESIGNS FOR STRESS REDUCTION

Glyn Bridgewater

southwater

Introduction

Take a peek inside this beautiful book, where you and your pencils are the last pieces of the puzzle...

Modern life can at times be stressful for all of us, from studying for exams and commuting long distances to coping with numerous digital distractions. It's no coincidence that people are turning to colouring books as a way of escaping hectic day-to-tasks for a brief time, and focusing on a creative activity that is entirely in the present. Colouring-in is a form of mindful meditation, where anxieties can be relieved by the simple act of picking up some pencils and enjoying the relaxing process of filling in the blanks.

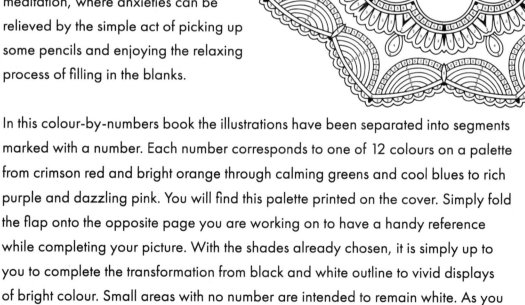

In this colour-by-numbers book the illustrations have been separated into segments marked with a number. Each number corresponds to one of 12 colours on a palette from crimson red and bright orange through calming greens and cool blues to rich purple and dazzling pink. You will find this palette printed on the cover. Simply fold the flap onto the opposite page you are working on to have a handy reference while completing your picture. With the shades already chosen, it is simply up to you to complete the transformation from black and white outline to vivid displays of bright colour. Small areas with no number are intended to remain white. As you slowly build up the design you will feel immense satisfaction at finishing the puzzle and bringing these wonderful artworks to life. The same picture without numbers is repeated on the left-hand page for you to complete using a colour palette entirely of your own choosing.

The soothing pictures inside these pages vary from spiritual mandalas to symmetrical patterns and swirling abstracts. Relax and unwind as your pencils glide over hypnotic shapes and kaleidoscopic images. Intriguing details within the drawings are brought to light as you colour them in piece by piece. Young and old alike will relish the joy of discovery in bringing these scenes to their full vibrant potential. Ten minutes each day will be enough to feel the therapeutic benefits – but you may find yourself drawn in for hours!

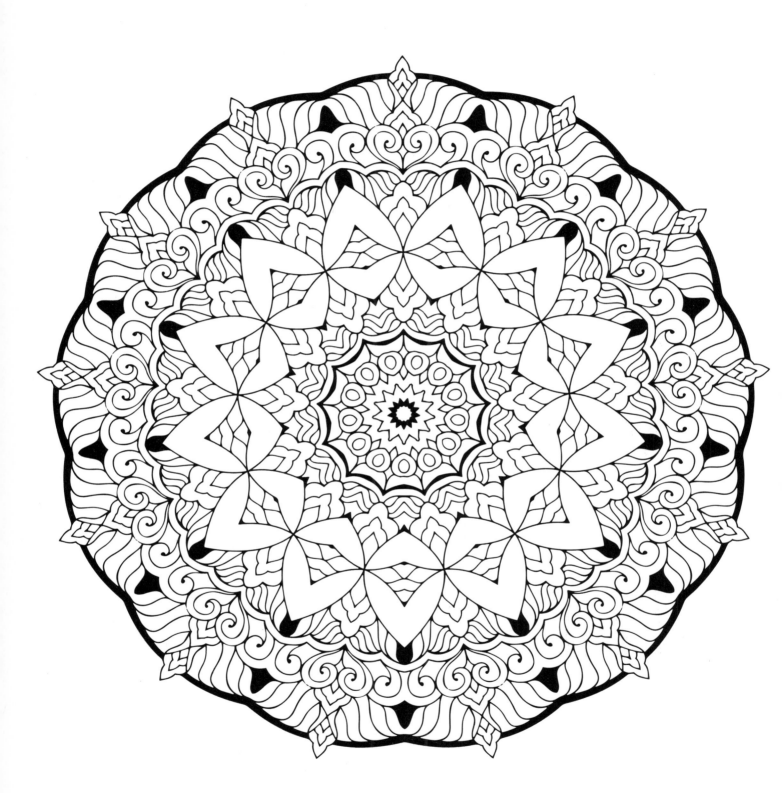

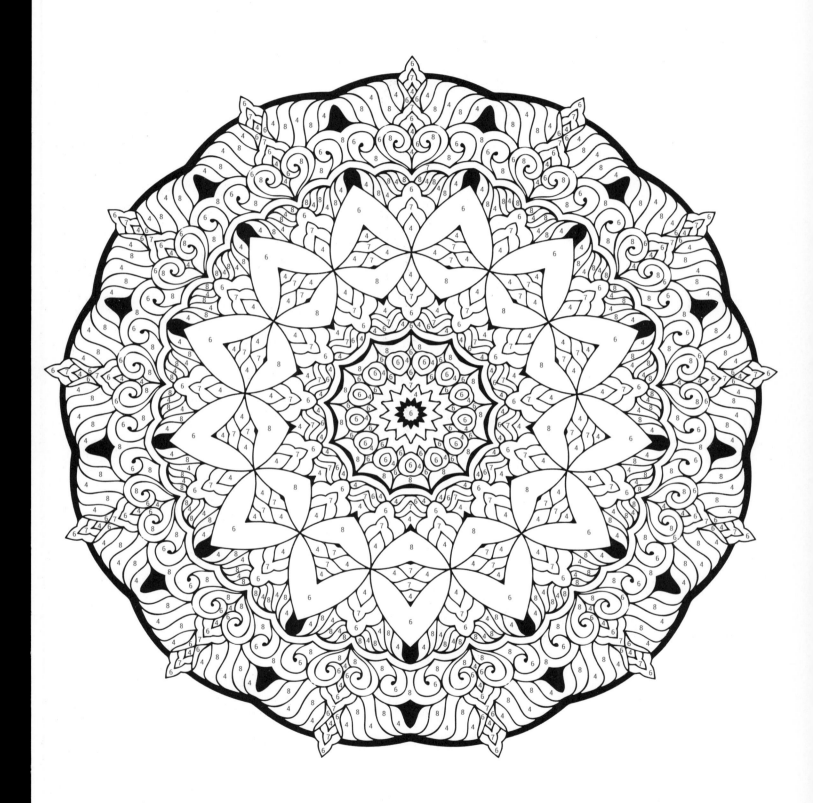

This edition published by Southwater, an imprint of Anness Publishing Limited
108 Great Russell Street, London WC1B 3NA
info@anness.com; www.annesspublishing.com
twitter @Anness_Books

© Anness Publishing Limited 2016

Publisher: Joanna Lorenz
Editorial Director: Helen Sudell
Designer: Glyn Bridgewater
Production Director: Ben Worley
Illustrations: Shutterstock

Publisher's Note
Although the information in this book is believed to be acccurate at the time of going to press neither
the author nor the publisher can accept any legal responsibility or liability for any errors or omissions
that may have been made.